Bats

by Matthew Hugo

Contents

Introduction	2
Bat Homes	6
A Bat Nursery	8
Bat Food	10
Vampire Bats	12
Conservation	14
Glossary	16

Pioneer Valley Educational Press, Inc.

INTRODUCTION

Bats live all over the world.
They live on every continent except for Antarctica.

Bats can fly but they are not birds.
Bats are mammals, like humans.
A bat's wings are made
of four long fingers that are webbed.
Bats are covered with fur
everywhere except for their wings.

Bats are the only mammals able to truly fly.

Most bats are **nocturnal**.
They sleep during the day and are active at night.
Many bats sleep hanging upside down.

Some people believe bats are blind.
This is not true!
Their eyes see best in the dark,
and most bats see only in black and white.

Most bats are nocturnal.

BAT HOMES

Some bats live alone in trees while others live in groups called **colonies**.

6

Many bats live in caves.
Caves are quiet and dark.
Bats that live in cold parts of the world, hibernate in the winter. Caves stay warm and make a good place for bats to hibernate.

A cave keeps bats warm and dry in the winter.

A BAT NURSERY

Female bats who are having babies
gather together to create a nursery.
There can be up to a million bats in one nursery.
A baby bat's eyes are closed only for the first day.
A baby bat has no fur for the first several days.
Within a week after its birth, the baby bat
is carried on the nightly hunts by its mother.
Like other mammals, a baby bat drinks milk
from its mother.

Just like humans, baby bats drink their mother's milk.

BAT FOOD

Almost all the bats that live in the United States eat insects. Bats fly around hunting for the insects. The bats find the insects using **echolocation**. Bats hear a buzzing sound and it helps them to locate the insect.

Many bats live in tropical areas, like the rain forest, where it is warm. These bats eat fruit.

Many trees are being cut down in the rain forest. Fruit bats are important to the regrowth of the rain forest. As they fly through the forest, they leave seeds in their droppings. These seeds help new trees to grow.

Many bats eat nectar from flowers or fruit from trees.

VAMPIRE BATS

Vampire bats feed only on blood.
Vampire bats are very small.
They are only about three inches long.
To obtain their food, they will feed on almost any warm-blooded animal
that is resting quietly. They make a small cut in the animal's skin with their teeth, and drink the blood. A Vampire bat's teeth are so sharp that the prey doesn't even feel the cut.

Bats can **transmit** diseases, such as rabies. This is not a common problem. Fewer than 40 people in the United States are known to have contracted rabies from bats during the past 40 years.

CONSERVATION

Some bats die because of natural **predators**. Most premature bat deaths are caused by the activities of people. Forty percent of the bats in the United States and Canada are endangered or may soon be endangered.

Bats can also die from **insecticides** used in farming. They can also die when their habitat is disturbed.

Most bats are important to humans because they help pollinate plants and spread seeds.
Bats also help reduce the number of bothersome insects. One bat can eat between 600 and 1,000 mosquitoes in just one hour.

Glossary

colonies: animals of the same kind living close together

echolocation: the sonarlike system used by bats and other animals to detect and locate objects by giving off a sound that reflects off the object and returns to the animal's ears

insecticide: a substance used for killing insects

nocturnal: active at night

predators: any animal that exists by preying upon other animals

transmit: to pass